Whispers of Starlight Butterflies

Poetry for the Soul

By Mara Elizari

SoulArt PRESS

WHISPERS OF STARLIGHT BUTTERFLIES

Poetry for the Soul

Cover art and inner graphics generated by AI
Cover and back cover design by Mara Elizari

Published by: Soul Art Press
Printed in the U.S.A
First Edition: 2025
ISBN: 979-8-9989303-0-0
For more information: www.soulartpress.com

DISCLOSURE
This poetry collection was edited with the help of AI assistance. AI tools were used to review text for grammar and stylistic suggestions, but all final decisions on content, language, and structure were made by Mara Elizari.

This book is for you.
To the loving presence
that moves through my breath
and guides the hand —
the silent light behind each word.

To you, dear reader,
who meets these pages with an open heart,
a kindred soul across the veil of time.

To those who have returned
to dust and stars,
and those still becoming —
wings, flame, and breath.

May these verses be a gift of the spirit,
a shimmer passed hand to hand,
from the unseen to the seen,
from one soul to another.

Epigraph

Before We Begin: Definitions of Soul

What the dictionary says:
soul *(n.)*: The spiritual or immaterial part of a human being, regarded as immortal.

What the mind thinks:
She is a radiant, bossy essence of my being. She says she's in the driver's seat. *(I'm not so sure.)*

What the Soul knows:
I Am What I Am. —M.E

What the poet whispers:
|soul *(n.)*: the immortal breath within the breath;

> the part of us
> > that remembers the stars.

Contents

Section 1: Whispers of the Soul

Section 2: Pilgrimage of Light

Section 4: Sacred Becoming

Section 5: Eternal Soul

In the Beginning:

One twilight, I glimpsed the stars
shimmering in a puddle
left behind by the summer rain.

Longing stirred within me
to leap into the heavens,
to dance among their silver fire.

So I leapt,
heart first, soul wide,
into that liquid sky.

But the stars dissolved,
slipping away
without even a whisper of farewell.

And I was left,
gently tethered
by gravity's quiet sorrow.

Still, I began to gather the falling stars,

to paint with the colors of starlight,

and weave my verses

from threads of celestial dust.

And so the journey unfolds,

on wings of wonder,

through the hidden sky.

How I Write Poetry

I sit down without a plan,

without rhyme,

or an outline.

Only a longing
to let something true flow.

Poetry is how I speak to myself

without judgment—

a sacred way of listening inward.

The words come before my thoughts form.

They arrive whole—

mysterious and sublime.

Who will read it?

Anyone brave enough to hear the truth,

anyone gentle enough to smile with it.

Audience or none,

I am a poet.

All else is obsolete.

Author's Introduction

I turned inward in the quiet aftermath of illness, the stillness that followed the storm of 2020. What began as a struggle became a sacred conversation between my soul and the silence.

Rather than let an invisible virus silence my spirit, I listened more deeply than ever. From that stillness, poetry emerged, colors came to life on canvases, and galaxies unfolded within me.

This book is a collection of such unfoldings. Each piece is a whisper from the soul, a glimpse into the beauty that rises when everything else fades away.

I offer these words to those who have wandered, been wounded, and sought answers, only to return to that quiet voice within. It knows the way, but we must become still enough to hear it.

Even what appears to break us may be a blessing in disguise as a threshold to something greater.

May these words remind you:

There is beauty in the breakdown,

light in the unknown,

and infinite grace in the soul's quiet song.

As Rumi said, *"The wound is the place where the light enters you."*

    Why write spiritual poetry

    after Rumi and Kabir have said it all?

    Perhaps they whisper unfinished poems

    into my dreams, gently nudging me,

    "Write. Write."

    For every soul has a voice of its own,

      and every story, its sacred telling.

Mara Elizari

Poems Are Like Butterflies

Poems arrive

on wings of Starlight—

like butterflies from another realm.

They dance

and flutter into my world,

landing softly on pages.

About This Book

Whispers of Starlight Butterflies is a sacred offering: poems gathered from the quiet spaces of the soul. Each verse carries the hush of stardust, the shimmer of transformation, and the subtle flight of remembrance. These pages are meant to be touched softly, as one would hold a butterfly—lightly, reverently, and with wonder.

Born of deep introspection, healing, and mystical longing, this collection is both deeply personal and profoundly universal. Through imagery of stars, wings, and divine light, Mara Elizari invites the reader into an intimate conversation with the unseen, where silence speaks, and the heart remembers its truth.

The spirituality woven throughout these poems is not a doctrine, but devotion. It is the flame that burns quietly within, the whisper that echoes in stillness, the light that rises when all else fades. Here, poetry becomes a lantern, a guide for those navigating grief, awakening, or the quiet unfolding of the self.

Themes of divine connection, soul resilience, sacred stillness, and the beauty of surrender are intricately woven through this tapestry like silver threads. With each turn of the page, readers are invited to return to the essence they have never truly lost.

This book is for dreamers, seekers, empaths, and mystics—for anyone who has ever felt the ache of the stars or the tenderness of unseen wings brushing their cheeks in the dark.

It is a tender invitation to remember who you are beneath the noise, and to listen when the stars begin to speak—a gentle calling from beyond the veil, asking you to remember your light, and to follow the starlit whisper all the way home to your soul.

Section 1: Whispers of the Soul

Silent Poem

The space between the breaths.
The silence between the words.
Emptiness and stillness—
all are One.

Twirling
in a sacred dance
of nothingness,
so magnificent
and serene.

I am in love
with knowing myself,
lost in God's love—
I am All That Is.

We Live in the Mind of God

We live in the mind of God.

We are His creation,

His thoughts and imagination.

The same Love that willed the Big Bang into an
explosion

forms my life,

creates joy,

and brings liberation.

God is awesome,

and I sing Him praises!

The Seed of a Rose

I am a velvet blue rose,
a flower of deep peace,
gentle and serene.

I am a luminous white rose,
the flower of spirit,
pure and sublime.

I am a radiant gold rose,
the flower of joy,
happy and free.

I am a blazing red rose,
a flower of passion,
fiery and bright.

I am all that…
and I don't know who I am—
perhaps just a seed
waiting to bloom.

The Shadow and the Light

"I want to be the power!"
the shadow screamed.
"I want to choose where to go,
when to rest,
and when to scare people off."

The Light replied gently:
"You want to be the winner?
Then why do you keep following me?"

The shadow sighed.
She frowned.
She cried:
"I tried!
But nothing worked...
Why can't I be myself
and live my own life?"

The Light smiled and whispered:
"You are yourself.

5

You have a life.

Stop comparing yourself to others.

You are important in your own way.

"Without you,"

the Light continued,

"I would burn all around—

no contrast,

no witness,

no choice.

Just the Empty Void."

"You bring balance to existence.

You are the shade,

the mystery,

the unknown.

Without you,

there is no free will.

Nothing to choose from.

No shadow,

no light."

The shadow looked up.

A softness entered her voice.
"So… I'm part of the story?"

The Light nodded:
"You are the fabric of life,
just as I am.

Two sides of one truth,
two siblings of one mother.

We exist to keep each other company,
So that the Universe can discover its own
reflection."

What Is Life?

I once thought

life was a pleasure to be felt.

Many times I struggled,

but to no avail.

I thought life was a school,

where lessons were everywhere.

Now, my life flows,

and the lessons are still coming.

My Duty

"I am here,"
I answered when God called.

"What is your duty?" He asked.
"To serve You, my Lord."

"I formed you,
shaped you,
and gave you dreams.
What is your duty?"
"To serve You," I replied.

"I gave you riches,
fame,
and success.
What is your glory?"
"To serve the One."
I gave you pleasures
and temptations of every kind.
What is your calling?"

   "To serve You, my Lord."

Manifesting

Life unfolds like an open book.

We add new chapters

and revise old dreams.

And simply hope:

When the final page turns,

we can exclaim—

"What a marvelous journey it was!"

Awakening

The shell of illusions cracks—
and I emerge.

Not new,
not old,
but eternal.

I awaken to the song
that has been playing all along—
soft, patient,
waiting for me to remember.

Walk gently—light follows every step that seeks.

Section 2: Pilgrimage of Light

Eternal Truth

I searched for healing
and delved deep into the dark earth.
Hot magma burned me,
but the pain remained.|

I flew above the stars,
into galaxies far away.
Cold stardust froze me,
but the pain remained.

I returned to Earth—
still without answers—
yet more at peace.
Not numb, just content,
I found myself in the middle,
letting go of judgment, fear, and illusions.

Only the essence of the soul truly exists.
Awareness brings peace,

as I surrender to the Divine.

I made peace with all that is.
The soul is a talented writer.
She now discovered a passion for painting.
Colors bring light
into this world of hidden good.

Despair heals old wounds
And illuminates new truths.
Life and death are merely illusions—
the veil is very thin.

Be true to yourself.
Embrace the unknown.
This body will not last forever.
The soul must live
to her highest dream.

All Is One

My Soul,
she knows the wisdom of ages.
She is wise
and eternally young.

Soon, time will reveal
who was right
and who was not.

Soon, we shall know the truth—
the only Truth, eternal.

There is only One God.
No other deities,
miracle makers,
or fortune tellers—
just the Holy One's presence within,
making a comeback to all
in visible, tangible,
undeniable ways.

No one will doubt.

No one will flee.

No one will despair.

All will rejoice.

All as One.

We will be together

and complete.

One Soul.

One humanity.

One kindness.

One grace.

So many good souls have perished from this Earth,

only to guide us from beyond.

This is the truth.

This is the comfort.

Only One God.

Only one human race.

Only one Earth.

Only one Becoming.

Love loves me.
Life loves me.

Nothing else is known.
No one says otherwise—
and if they do,
it is not valid.

Only the Soul knows.
Only my Soul do I trust.
The divine essence resides within me.
Only that is eternal.
Only that is real.

Matrix illusions run rampant,
creating chaos,
endless temptations,
fears and delusions—
all vain and obsolete.
None will last.

None will endure:
the test of time,
the test of famine,
the test of pandemics,
the tests of war and grief.

Only Love is eternal.
Only Soul-life exists.
All else is just a fleeting moment
of untruth and struggle.

Where do I go from here
but to Heaven?
It long awaits me,
but I intend to bring it down,
here,
to this Earth,
to my sacred ground,
to my ancestors,
my descendants,
to all times and places
where life is valid,

where love flows freely—

through the hearts of brave warriors,

merciful healers,

nurturing mothers,

loyal defenders of faith,

precious children,

all living beings,

sprouting beings,

still beings.

All that He created

has a place and a merit of its own.

Do not forget this simple truth

in the caravans of lives,

in the dreadful locks of fate.

Simple but genuine:

Who you are

and who you shall become—

the choice is yours.

Yet all is written,

and all is numbered.

There is nowhere to run,
nowhere to hide.
Only dive deep
into your own being.

Seek refuge in your sanctuary,
where you meet God
deep within your sorrows
and forgotten grief.

He illuminates you
with everlasting glory.
He embraces you gently.
He loves you, child —
do not despair.
He is by your side
and all around.

See Him in the flight of a dove.
See Him in a child's smile.

See Him in the heavens.

See Him in the Earth.

See Him in yourself.

See Him beyond what can be seen.

Trust He is there —

when nothing is seen,

where nothing yet exists,

and where all is forgotten.

Where All is One.

Dreams and Attachments

Sometimes great things come from great pain:

Transforming pain into wisdom,

desperation into gratitude.

Giving thanks for all that was given,

I have come to know peace

and let go of what was long forgiven.

Somewhere, my other version

runs barefoot in the rain.

I am her,

proclaiming glory to the Lord,

cheerful when roses bloom,

when squirrels steal my strawberries,

and a single blade of grass

breaks through concrete.

Letting go of attachments is not
easy. But when dreams are freed—
without expectation—
we can find true peace.

Paradise

Sing, sing—
for you have endured too much pain.

Dance, dance—
for all is in flux.

Where you have been,
where you are headed,
are old, forgotten stories.

Be amazed, traveler—
for somewhere beyond,
rainbows bloom.

Perhaps there,
in the blueness of the heavenly void,
you will meet unicorns,
dance with fairies,
and never grow old.

Forgive yourself.

You are already home.

Welcome to paradise.

Feeling Lost

Somewhere between the virus attacks
and the endless storm of world news,
I lost myself.

Endlessly seeking solace,
endlessly searching
for a new version of me.

What else can make sense,
if not the growing pains of existence?

We are scarred by our life stories,
only to find peace within.

The Journey

Three thousand miles away—
cold North, gray skies,
nowhere to find refuge.

I turned within,
to golden light,
to the beauty of pure spirit,
where God is always present.

What we see and touch
is a transient dream.

The soul's refuge lies beyond it all.
Keep moving, traveler—
descending and ascending
until your timeless home is found.

Grateful Heart

I am beautiful and comely,
sacred and human.

God created me with sweetness and strength.
He formed me in His secret chambers,
pouring His abundant love and joy into my soul.
I am forever grateful for His kind ways.
He taught me great lessons—
oh, so painful, but so wise!

How can I repay You, Lord,
for Your mercy and gifts?
I am so humble,
and yet so proud to be Your servant.
You never abandon,
reject, or judge.
You are the most loving Parent,
caring and amazingly kind.
How wondrous are Your deeds!
I am in awe.

Embracing the Journey

I have embraced
the science of welcomes and goodbyes,
sorrows and joy,
wisdom and love.

The eternal motion of All That Is,
the endless unfolding of life's mysteries.

Don't worry about your destination,
traveler of time.

Just be yourself
on this sacred journey.

Peace and Joy

Sweetness and love—
all gifts from God,
gifts from beyond.

Do not be fooled by external beauty—
the world is not what it seems.
Trust only your true Self;
the higher part of you knows the truth.

When sadness comes,
follow its trail to the origin.
There, in the truth of abandonment,
you may suddenly feel peace,
understanding how it was meant to be.

You'll see how separation wounded your being.
Let go of the illusion of being alone—
separation from the Source is temporary,
it was never meant to last.

In the grip of primordial fear,
you fight your way to the Light.
And oneness becomes accessible,
attainable by default.

Try and you may fail.
Believe—and you shall achieve.
Believing is seeing --
seeing the true nature of reality.

Simple pleasures
give way to enlightened peace:
Growing flowers,
gazing at stars,
creating new worlds
on the canvas of the old.

All is meant to bring beauty
into this creation,
and manifest godliness
in myriad subtle ways.

Be yourself, my friend,
your journey is just beginning.

Allow yourself to embark
on the path to becoming all.
The insatiable beauty within you
is growing,
bursting into holy flame
where sadness is no more.

Laughter and serenity
birth new outcomes
of hope and surrender
to the Divine Will.

Living without fear
is the path of the brave,
those who know the truth
of divine adventures.

You shall be one with the Lord again.

Until then,

embrace your true nature

and be at peace.

Light Keeper

I carry a flame—

small but steady—

through the endless corridors of night.

I did not ask for this burden,

but it is mine to bear,

and I carry it with quiet grace.

When the night howls,

and shadows scream,

I tend my flame,

and I pray

not for myself,

but for all travelers lost in the dark.

Section 3: COSMIC EMBRACE

Every galaxy holds a memory of your spark.

Held in the breath of stars, you return to the Infinite.

When No One Listens

When no one listens,
God whispers in my ear:
"I am here."

Do not be afraid, my child.
All fear is an illusion.

Go within,
where truth resides.
You will find Me there,
always.

Amid the storms,
the lonely days,
the grief for what was lost—
know this:
You are protected.

You are loved.

You are never forgotten.

What seems like a loss

will become a great source

of joy and serenity

in due time.

Don't count days,

count blessings

and hope.

They are your treasures, Divine.

Don't cry over dreams

that didn't come true;

your perception was off—

that's all.

Be free to receive

the most wondrous gifts

and still

be the dreamer.

You are the eternal Soul.

Do not give up.
Do not change your course.

You have accomplished great things
you've already forgotten.
There's no one else
who could have walked your path,
so give yourself a big hug.

Your gifts to others
weren't always received.
You were disappointed.
But you are free
to cherish yourself.

Gifts are also meant for you.
You forgot
you deserve them
more than anyone.
So love yourself,

before others do.

You will receive
and then share—
freely,
not out of duty,
but as your birthright.

You deserve
great love,
joy,
serenity,
appreciation,
safety,
respect,
and peace.

Forget their cruel words,
And insecurities.
They have wounds to heal.
Let them seek their own salvation.

The one worthy of you

will not despair

to approach you in love,

to bring you somewhere

where lovebirds are heard,

rainbows bloom,

and mighty trees wear

blossom dresses like brides.

Because you, too,

are Divine.

You are free

to love God

and yourself.

Compass of the heart

So many times I've doubted—
the journey, the worth, the outcome.
So many times I've been afraid
that I'd never return home.

But somehow, a spark remains,
a flicker of trust
in the middle of the storm.

I carry within me
an invisible compass,
pointing inward
to the true north of my soul.
The world swirls with confusion,
but I no longer chase answers.

I've come to rest

Within the question itself,

and I've found peace

in not knowing everything.

The compass of the heart

always finds its way

when silence is allowed to speak.

Space Between Worlds

There is a space between words,
between worlds,
between who I was,
and who I am becoming.

It is not a place you can visit;
it opens only when you are still.

It does not welcome noise,
only the breathless hush
of awe.

In that space,
time folds,
pain transforms,
and all my past selves gather
not to haunt me,
but to honor me.

They lay their burdens down
and whisper:
"We are proud of you.
You chose the truth.
You chose light.
You chose You".

Burnt Offerings

I gave you my words,
my prayers,
my most secret dreams.

You set them on fire,
and I watched them burn
silent and wide-eyed,
like a child watching
paper boats disappear.

But even in ashes
there is wisdom.
Even in endings,
a sacred spark remains.

From the ruins
of what I once hoped for,
a new temple is rising—
built not of illusions,
but of raw truth, earned grace,

and unwavering self-love.

This time,
I do not beg for it to last.
I bless the flames
and walk forward,
bathed in light.

Sublime

Golden leaves.
Blue skies.
White clouds—
a keyhole in the sky.

A woman walks her path
among the trees.
The path is straight
and leads to the keyhole.

A subtle, simple truth
is greater
than elaborate illusions.
Lies are not born of Heaven.

That which is unseen—
and utterly sublime—
guides her gently
along her path.

It supports her
with quiet strength.

She does not see it—
but feels it
with the knowing of her soul.
And all the faith
she gathers along the way,
she gives freely
to All That Is.

Dreamers of the Light

Somewhere far beyond the veil,
dreamers weave worlds of wonder.

They remember the ancient songs,
even when they walk in silence.

They hold the ember of stars in their hands
and scatter radiant light across the dark fields of
earth.

We are the dreamers—
brave, broken, and luminous.

We dream
because we remember
where we come from.

Star Traveler

Who are you, O wanderer of skies?

I am a traveler among the stars,
a seeker of forgotten dreams.

I ride the rivers of stardust,
chasing whispers from ancient worlds—
lost songs of Creation,
echoing in my soul.

I do not know the map,
but I trust the melody of the stars.

It leads me home.

Star Gatherer

So I became a star gatherer:

Catching falling stars,

collecting Stardust,

weaving colors of Starlight

into the Northern Lights fantasy.

Words are flowing,

As gentle hands care for the sick,

And loving eyes engage

in the world's action drama.

Hooray!

I did it! I caught enough stars

to make the Earth happier.

I painted so many canvases with gorgeous

colors not of this world.

I transformed specks of stardust

into poetic words,

enough to build the bridge to heaven.

The world is now better,

or perhaps not yet,

but I did my part,

And that is all that matters.

Fly, My poems, Fly

Fly, my poems, fly
on the wings of Starlight
over high mountains,
across wide oceans,
above gardens of wonder.

Flutter into dreams,
into waiting hearts,
so they may feel complete.

Section 4: Sacred Becoming

*In the stillness of unknowing, a new self
begins to bloom.*

Singing Rocks

Why do rocks sing with the whispers of ancient
tales?

Why do rainbows keep on traveling across the sky,

unfurling their vibrant colors?

Why do little puppies never seem to grow old,

and roses bloom in beauty

yet never truly die?

Because all is eternal— a cycle without end.

From where the seed comes,

it has already shed its petals

only to begin anew—vibrant and full of life.

Such is the lovely dance of life:

What comes into being must depart,

and what is born must return

to the embrace of its origins.

The sinner must confess,

the saint is anointed,

and eventually, they too pass away.

In the end, white chess pieces

rest in harmony beside the black ones.

No battles waged,

just a serene unity,

and the quiet promise of peace.

Sacred Dreamers

I know no sorrow—
only a sense of humanity drifting apart.

So many human races,
so many temptations.
Matrix illusions never sleep,
creating new disguises.

Even the brave
get caught in the traps.
But with the soul's eternal fire,
they awaken to a deeper truth.

Through brokenness and grief,
they forge a new kind of being:
Light Warriors.

They walk through darkness with grace and
purpose,
refusing to sink into the abyss.

They tame their dragons
with the power of pure love.

Sacred Dreamers,
planting rainbows in barren lands,
birthing miracles through gentleness—
untouched by darkness,
radiant and divine.

They dream the world anew.

Poem from My Heart

From my heart to yours,

many blessings sail through this world.

From my heart to yours,

much love and peace.

Our souls know—

the mind does not comprehend.

But the guidance from on high

is forging new bridges.

Nothing can stand in the way

of an eternal bond

designed by God Himself.

No one can ruin the trust—

for we are One,

undivided in spirit.

Where you go, I am there;

where I lie to rest,

you whisper sweet lullabies.

What does it matter
if you run?

It is your mind
that becomes afraid—
not understanding
what Divine love is:
Love that transcends time and space,
love that forgives,
sings,
and dances with the Universe.

What does it matter if we are separated?
Our souls know—
the moment of unity will arrive:
Pure, sweet,
and absolutely Divine!

Peace

No worrying, crying, or feeling upset,

No excessive bursts of gladness or fiery anger.

Just a serene sense of peace enveloping your spirit.

Tend to the delicate garden within you,

allow the roses to bloom,

each petal is a reminder of beauty in simplicity.

The world is but an intricate illusion—

don't get consumed by it.

Instead, embrace the stillness of peace;

for in this tranquility, you truly belong,

exactly where you are needed most.

Hidden light

Sacred Light,

hidden deep within—

My inner sanctuary,

my essence, my soul—

it shines bright.

But at times,

dark clouds of despair,

toxic people

and sad news

dim the Light,

leaving me vulnerable

and unsure of myself.

The pain of darkness

pushed me to explore ways of salvation,

but to no avail.

And I returned to the land of my soul,

hidden deep within.

The eternal flame flickering,

still bright and going strong,

"You are still here!"

I exclaimed with joy.

"I thought I lost you;

I thought you were gone."

"No", said the Light.

"I am always here.

I am you,

and you know it better than any guru.

Why search for answers,

for joy, for peace,

in all the wrong places,

outside yourself?

Seek me out,

and you will find your way,

never to feel lost again.

Fill my heart with the warmth of your love,

and I will shine forever—

radiant, vibrant,

and overflowing with joy

beyond anything I have ever felt."

So there we sat,

tears streaming down our cheeks,

laughter bubbling forth.

Oh, how I laughed in delight,

alongside my beautiful Light:

My dearest friend,

the wisest of teachers,

and the most loving being

I have ever known.

My hidden Light knows it all.

Forgiving,

gentle,

serene—

it never fades,

never leaves.

The deeper I go,

the brighter it shines.

It is my sacred Source,

my blessing,

my heavenly paradise.

Divine Plan

You know the deal isn't over
if the soul is still evolving.
There is no limit to perfection—
I am one with all of Creation.

I've risen above trivialities,
The illusions and fleeting perceptions.
My body still aches,
and my mind races with thoughts and reflections.

But the soul is at peace and content.
She knows no fear.
"I love you,"
She whispers softly.
"You are doing fine, my dear."

The soul is untouched
By the agony of the flesh.

She only knows her path
and cares about her ascension.

"Just how long can I endure?"
I asked, losing strength.
"You are perfectly fine, my dear,"
The soul answered.
"All is well, as it should be
according to the Divine Plan."

Phoenix Rising

Who are you, fiery bird,
blazing through the heavens with golden wings?
I asked your name—
and heard my own.

I share your essence,
yet we exist in different realms.
You are the searing flame.
I am the soul that ascends.

I burn to ashes,
and fly again—
each sorrow becomes a feather,
each dream ignites a spark.

I am the glorious bird reborn from flames,
the eternal wanderer crowned with fire.
I am Phoenix, rising from the depths of despair.
I am Mara, reborn to rise even higher!

When life stops making sense

When life stops making sense,

I start desperately searching for answers.

Then, the heart bleeds,

and tears roll down my face,

dripping onto a canvas as colorful dots,

burning the paper

with sacred words.

Don't try

to find all the answers,

for an unsolved mystery

can unravel the fabric of creation.

Section 5: Eternal Soul

Listen closely—your soul still remembers how to sing.

I Am the Sacred Soul

I am the sacred soul
radiating the sacred Light.

My body —
the holy garment,
while my mind believes it is in charge.

How silly the workings of the mind can be—
confused, distracted, and obsolete.

The Soul knows her purpose
and is in the driver's seat.

I Did Not Know

I do not know who I am.

Identity crisis.

Simply put—

I am no one.

I am many.

I am lost and confused

All is in vain.

Attempts to recover

are subtle at best.

I want to be me,

but I am now new.

They say I am a better version

of what I used to be.

How do I accept that truth?

Illusions are rampant.

The Matrix is ever strong --

throwing a curveball.

I feel lost.

But deep within,

a quiet voice whispers:

"You are uniquely you.

You are one and the same—

always was, is, and will be.

Embrace compassion for all parts of yourself—

those who have been hurt, betrayed,

or cast into oblivion.

Each moment and struggle

has been a necessary thread

in the tapestry for your journey.

Allow it all to be.

Let the music flow freely,

butterflies dance gracefully in the sunlight,

and angels carry out their sacred work.

In this moment, just be.

Simply be

Your true Self."

No Pain, No Gain

Covid came and brought me pain.

No pain, no gain, they say.

Tired of walking in pain,

tired of counting sorrows,

I hid so deep within

my aching heart—

and there, I found God.

In the darkest hour of misery,

the speckles of hope shine brightly.

Feeling His love within,

hope exploded like a supernova.

Pain turned into grey hair,

sorrows hidden in new wrinkles.

I paint the grey with gorgeous red

and adorn the face with lovely colors.

The scars are covered with glitter.

I dance my sacred dance

in beautiful, flowing garments.

New poems emerged,

and new paintings are shining.

I am no longer the old self.

I have become the Divine.

Eternal Dance

I am the star.
The point of all beginnings.

No life, no death,

no sense, no math—

I just am.

Thousands of worlds pass through me,

millions of years traverse me.

I am Stardust, solar clouds,

A black hole and the explosion of a supernova.

I am All. I am nothing.

I am All That Is, Was, and Ever Will Be.

Such strange awareness is nonsense,

some will say.

What does it matter

if you don't exist?

It is just Me.

So many lives, so many plans.
Unrealized dreams,
Unfinished wars,
Conquests and triumphs—
All these do not exist.
Only I,
my visions, my dreams,
and my desires.

To evolve. To create.
To know myself.
I expand and withdraw,
paint and erase,
write endless symphonies,
dance in the starlight.

Who are you?
Just a traveler.
Who am I?
The point of singularity,
non-existent matter,

the dance of photons
and waves.

Galaxies are my toys,
grand designs are my puzzles.

What are you?
Who do you know?

No one else exists—
just you and me—
in the eternal, sacred dance
of All That Is.

I Am a Mystic

I am a mystic
and a channeler of Light.

My poems are not mental ramblings
or emotional outbursts—
they are dreams made of heavenly dew,
Starlight fairies,
Starseed butterflies,
spirits and angels,
speaking gently through the keys
and taking new shapes on canvas,
flowing with grace.

Declaration of Formless Art

As Spirit has no shape or form,

do not expect my poetry

to fit within rigid structures,

follow rules

or cling to familiar styles.

As the Spirit flows,

so do my poems—

like skies repainted with a rainbow

after each rain.

My paintings are simply colors,

living lives of their own—

unspoken revelations,

longing to enter our world.

So I let the words fly sweetly,

and the colors pour gently,

to let the world know:

Spirit has arrived.

In Gratitude

I want to thank my family and friends for their
loving presence and encouragement.
Deep thanks to all my teachers—seen and unseen—
for their unconventional wisdom, endless humor,
and unwavering support.

A Note from the Author

Thank you for joining me on the journey through
Whispers of Starlight Butterflies.

If these poems resonated with your soul
or brought a moment of brightness to your day,
I would be deeply grateful if you shared your
thoughts with others.
Even a few kind words in a review
can help this book find its way to more hearts.

With gratitude,
Mara Elizari

About the Author

Mara Elizari is a physician and poet, a healer of both body and soul. She walks between the worlds of medicine and mysticism, where the language of science meets the whispers of Spirit. Through years of service and introspection, she has witnessed the tender ache of being human and the quiet strength that rises through it.

Her poetry is born of sacred stillness, shaped by spiritual awakening, and a longing to illuminate the soul's journey. In her verses, the seen and unseen converge: light rises from shadow, and silence becomes song.

Whispers of Starlight Butterflies is her heartfelt offering—an invitation into grace, wonder, and the radiant mystery within.

Closing Prayer: Wings of Light

Fly, my poems, fly,

on the wings of ancient Light,

through realms unseen,

where soul and star entwine.

Touch the hearts of wanderers,

whisper to the weary and the lost,

kindle their memories of the Divine,

remind them:

They are never alone.

Carry my love to distant shores,

my prayers into the dreaming sky,

my hopes into gardens yet to bloom.

You are not merely words—

you are vessels of Spirit,

feathers of Eternity,

fragments of my soul
returning to the Source.

Go now, gentle offerings,
bless the world in ways I may never know.

I send you forth with wonder,
I send you forth with peace,
I send you forth with Light.

Mara Elizari

Future Releases from Soul Art Press

Coming Summer–Fall 2025 and Beyond

🦋 Butterfly Musings
A whimsical, winged collection of poetic notes, letters, and musings from Aurora the Butterfly Muse.

🦋 Inner Light
A soul poetry collection illuminated with the author's original paintings and visual meditations.

🦋 Wings of Wonder
A poetic storybook for children—featuring mystical creatures, starlit adventures, and animal wisdom.

🦋 Inspired by the Bible
An art and poetry calendar exploring sacred texts through a lens of beauty, light, and reflection.

🦋 Inspired by Nature
A seasonal art and poetry calendar—and coordinating stationery—celebrating the living spirit of the earth.

All titles are published by Soul Art Press:
A sanctuary for poetic vision and creative light.

www.ingramcontent.com/pod-product-compliance
Lightning Source LLC
Chambersburg PA
CBHW031217120626
46545CB00003B/885